This is Hank. He is

And this is Lin. She is a zin.

1

Hank had a long, thin chin.
But he couldn't see his chin.

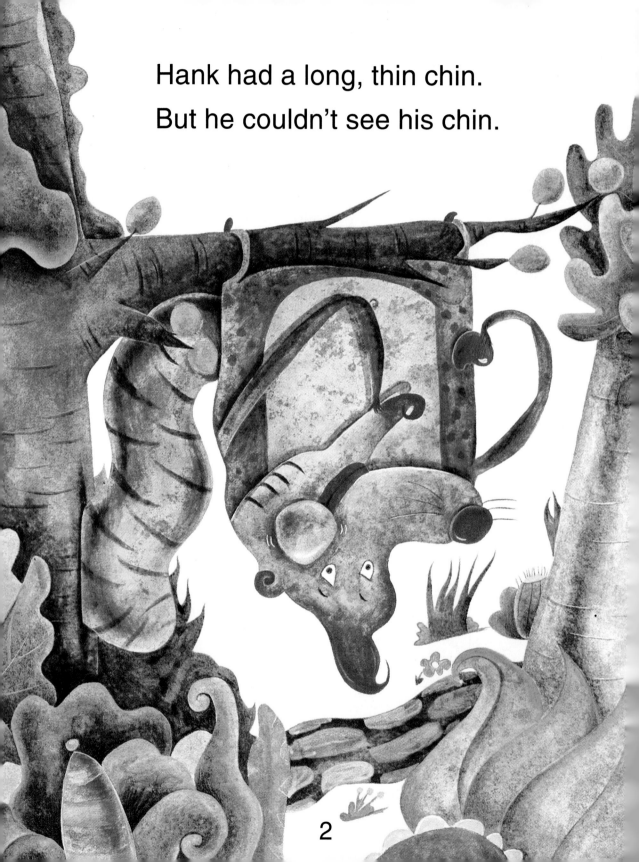

Lin had a long, thin chin too.
And she couldn't see her chin.

3

"Do I have a chin, Lin?" said Hank.

"If you jump down, then I will see," said Lin.

"Do I have a chin?" said Lin.

"If you jump up, then I will see," said Hank.

"You do have a chin!" said Lin.

"It's a long, thin chin."

"And you have a chin, Lin!" said Hank.
"Yours is long and thin too."

"Thank you for seeing my chin," said Hank.
"And I have YOU to thank, Hank,"
she called back to him.